THE WORLD PUSHES BACK

THE WORLD PUSHES BACK

POEMS

Garret Keizer

Library of Congress Cataloging in Publication Data
is on file at the Library of Congress, Washington, DC

Cover photo courtesy of Jake Mosher; *Winter* © 2018
Designed by Lisa C. Tremaine

For Kathy and Sarah, always,

and in loving memory

of James Hayford

and Howard Frank Mosher

CONTENTS

TRAVELING LIGHT

The older I get the less I'm bothered
by seeming incongruity.
I read the Gospel of Mark listening
to Billie Holiday. A young man
runs away naked from the Garden of Gethsemane
and Billie sings, "I'm traveling light."
Eventually you find the rhyme
for every word. The night
is coming—perhaps that's why—
the color that goes with everything.

WHEN THE SNAKE BECAME A MAN

1.

When the snake became a man,
he couldn't stop swallowing
one rat after another until
he became so large he couldn't
constrict his prey. He hired
a number of smaller snakes
not men or barely so to strangle
the rats for him and a surgeon
to make an opening in his tail
over which he wore a velvet hat
when not extruding his meals.

2.

When the elk became a man,
he found he wanted longer horns
and took it as a sign from God
that horn-grow cream appeared
around the same time as his wish.
He dipped the tips of his antlers
faithfully into the jars, having
first glued their bottoms to his sink—
it was just too awkward otherwise.
Soon his rack became so high
he could not raise his head
so bought a titanium crane
that followed him on little wheels,
took pictures, and sorted his socks.

3.
When the whale became a man,
it was really no big deal, the whale
already a Sea World celebrity,
people used to seeing him in a tux.
The orca bit would have to go,
of course, the cant about his not being
such a killer. No, he liked to kill
well enough, it was his culture
and he wasn't going to be ashamed
of it any more than werewolves were
of theirs. He thought he'd write a song.

4.
When the man became a man,
his dog became despondent,
having been a man himself
for quite some time. "A fine
thing to do at our stage of life,"
he said. Best friends with the man
for many years, he understood
the strange things likely to happen
when a man became a man.
The TV would go for one thing
and who knew what else after.
He wasn't about to wait around
and watch the transformation.
He packed up his bones
in their matching bone cases,
dusted off his real-estate license,
and headed down the road.

THE STARS ARE NEAR

The stars are near,
and it struck me how near
tonight, how superstitious I have been
to take their exponential distances on faith,
like a man dubious about driving a nail
because he's heard of empty space
between the molecules
in the hammer's head.
They are near, the stars.
They will always be
near. I have neighbors
whose porch lights are more distant.
A man who believes himself estranged
from his father, because they quarreled
when he was young,
sees the day when he is no longer
young, and no longer estranged,
and no more distant from the nearest star
than from his final breath.
He vows, as I do,
that he will not have his distances
dictated to him any more.

MORNING

Everything is better in the morning,
the first pretzel
and the first written word,
the first dung dropping
like a ripened apple,
the bowels as clear
as the song of a bird.

And if we turn to face each other,
warm and ready to be tasted
as the day's first bread,
that is better too—
if later on we fall asleep,
you might say that even night
is better in the morning.

Only you are unimproved,
as sweet before in darkness
as afterward
in light.

HELL AND LOVE

Hell is always grander to paint
Than the bliss of a resurrected saint;
More fun to show the lecher's doom,
Tits and ass in the flicking gloom.

Yet love inspires more than hate,
A head caressed than on a plate,
And even should his colors wash,
I'd put Chagall in front of Bosch.

The Passion is a painter's dream,
With hell and love a single theme—
The human body stripped to show
A death both merciful and slow.

SIMPLE MACHINES

Most of mechanics he learned
in his body, most of the simple machines,
the lever in the length of his arm,
the incline in the pivot of his foot.

Who knows where he found the pulley,
but he must have had bodily reasons
for calling his most physical act
after eating "a screw."

Mastering these, he found
their most ingenious uses
in taking a body apart,
the wheel that made him footloose
turned to breaking feet;
the arm-inspired handle
ratcheting the rack.

His pulley pulled his victim
twisting off the floor.
As far as he could get
from making love, he screwed.

Image of God, he broke it,
holding up a crucifix to eyes
that grasped it for the first time,

while backwards he fell
beyond all comprehension,
before the simple machines,
before the invention of hope.

FIREHOUSE

Right away I know
that the real estate sign
outside the firehouse
is a prank,

stolen and stuck there
by some imp
when the rest of the town
was sleeping.

The firemen would never
sell their house,
having raised it themselves
only a year ago,

and weren't we inside
as lately as last month,
eating hotdogs and watching
the kids clamber

over the engines?
So many handholds
for their little fists,
and the firehouse is one

of ours, a thing to grasp
as the darkness falls
on courts and churches
dry as tinder.

TWO TREES

Two trees too close for my design to let
light in between and make a grove effect,
a maple and a thicker ash, tête-à-tête
above the shady floor, both straight, the defect
of their nearness the only defect I could find.
But as I wondered whether to cut or keep,
I wondered what within each wooden mind
would seem more treely true or rooted deep:
that being close, they were protected, braced,
a proof against the loneliness of gales,
or that their upper branches interlaced
were to the trunks the shadow bars of jails.
Say "both," but both is not a thing you can do.
The saw demands to know which is more true.

LEAFLETING WITH FATHER CASTLE

We each took a side of Newport's main street
and roughly equal shares of "Nuclear War
in Vermont," which scaled the thermonuclear heat
of bombs against our most familiar star.
Sun warms this cold northeast as slightly as
the awful chances were beginning then
to touch our neighbors. The strange thing was
they took our pamphlets. Only a few of the men
waved us away.

              Father Castle joked
with them all—never a death's-head smirk.
A paunchy, balding businessman he poked
below the vest. "Do you know how these bombs work,
what fallout means? Your hair starts falling out,
you grow this great big gut . . ." Less point than nerve,
his dialectic? Yet physicists have no doubt
the shortest path in heaven is a curve.

Our seed all sown, some choked by the thistles,
some on hard cement, flapping like a dead
dove's wings blown with all the factory whistles,
we headed back to church beneath a red
sky, a better-red-than-hopeless sky,
to drink a cold beer in the parish house,
where we'd said prayers and since have said good-bye.

Did we really think we'd save the world? Of course
not. Jesus saves. We only hoped that we might
help, that we might prove more than helpless men,
and it does help me to think of him tonight
and how the world seemed so worth saving then.

DIVINE COMEDY

1.
Hell is eternal publication.
The damned never write a word
except their names at book signings,
never read anything but reviews
of books they can't remember writing.

They are stuck on the radio for ages,
talking about their goddamn books—
so long they forget they're on the air.
They call themselves on the call-in line
and ask, "So how did you get published?"

2.
Heaven is eternal publication.
The redeemed never write a word
not quickened by their inscribing:
"For Jane Doe, who graced this event,
and is the truth I sought by writing."

They are guests on the radio for ages,
talking to God, who just loved the book—
so long they forget they're on the air.
Again they drift to ground and find
their first acceptance, too good to be true.

BEATRICE

Midway this way of life we're bound upon
I woke to find myself in a dark wood . . .

I do not know what Dante's was
but this would do
to raise hell in anyone's heart:

the hunch that maybe you have never
really loved another soul
in your entire life,

that it was all and always about you
and who you wanted to be,
who you wanted
to seem like, and how
you wanted to feel,

nothing but bluff, need, and narcissism.
The earth would surely open
under you right there and then

but for remembering that one,
that whoever-it-is you would run to,
crying with this awful knowledge.

THE NEIGHBORS

When a man and woman built their house
on the hill behind mine, thus ruining
forever the satisfaction I took
in seeing no house but mine
in any direction,
I felt cheated and bitter.
I live at the foot of the hill,
I thought, and any time they wish,
they can peer into my yard.

But they were peerless people,
most times quiet as the trees
they had not cut, their voices murmurs
in the wind, their jackets flashing
colored wings among the branches.
The woman gave birth to a son,
who calls my name cycling down the road
as though I were his long-lost friend.

So I live at the foot of the hill,
and any bitter man who would climb it,
meaning my neighbors harm,
must first get past me.

WIND TRUMPS THE WORLD

Wind that takes the dead
wood from the trees,
that makes our willow drop
its dry branches like a busted thief
emptying his pockets onto the ground,
that tells our flag that flying
is not the same as flirting,
it's a serious affair and nothing glorious
is what it's cracked up to be—
wind trumps the world today.
Leaves, torn wrappers tear by,
commuters late for their train,
hats lift and slips show, umbrellas
once as upright as lollipops
flip end over end in the gale,
while garbage lids rise
gyroscopic off their knocked over cans,
mutter screw it there's got to be more
to life than this and roll down the road—
and the road, a metropolis in Rapture,
millions of grains of dust gone up
to meet those wild beckoning arms.
Every chink in our reprobate house
pants its confession now,
and the screen door, finally
at its limit, flies open like a secretary
backhanding her blowhard boss.

WHEN YOU'RE GONE

The tablecloth is always crooked
when you're gone—overnight
the whole kitchen table puts on
the costume of a bag lady,
its hems awry, full of empty
bottles and scraps of torn mail.

Our daughter is better behaved.
She rises solemnly for school,
no arguments or dillydallying
while I follow your careful instructions
for packing her lunchbox.
She kisses me often,
but I know as much as love
this is bereavement;

this is her quiet laboring
under the dark spell I too feel,
attending her good-night prayers
then working till the wee hours
so I can fall asleep, wishing
we could sleep the time away
"till Mommy comes home."

DUBLIN

The street with the sorry hotels,
where we decided not to stay,
is the street you've lived on
since the Book of Kells.

The video cameras trained
on the alleys, doors, and halls
record the special effects
of our historic stealing steps.

Mornings we strolled down
O'Connell Street, past big
Jim Larken's outspread arms
and his great ironic line:

"The great appear great
because we are on our knees."
But the small, they still look
small beneath our feet.

THE DETAILS

If God is love and God
is in the details, then love
is in the details too—

is in the way I trim
these crabgrass tassels
after mowing your father's lawn.

Two kids kiss
on a dark back porch
and a lawn gets mowed

thirty years later.
Love makes the world
go round. Love makes the world.

OLDSMOBILE

I'm sorry for the passing of the Oldsmobile.
I never owned one but my father did.
"This is not your father's Oldsmobile,"
the last-ditch advertisements said.
(It certainly wasn't, though I looked to be sure.)
Next thing the Oldsmobile was dead.

It was the only car that Malcolm X
would drive. When Alex Haley had a mind
to light up, Malcolm X
told him, neither fuming nor resigned,
"That would make you the first to smoke in this car,"
an honor Haley wisely declined.

My father, who never smoked a day in his life,
liked Malcolm's righteous white and black.
He liked that photo that appeared in *Life*:
armed papa poised to give it back.
I doubt King's dream speech moved him more.
He never wanted a Cadillac.

MARX'S FAMILY

As sure its kind would disappear
as Darwin was that man evolved,
old Mohr enjoyed his nuclear family—

a short nap's respite from *Kapital*,
a chapter or two of *Ivanhoe*
aloud to the girls before supper.
He watched the old forms passing
like casserole dishes down to Jenny
from his place at the head of the table,

foresaw the suitors who would come,
the part he'd play of bourgeois papa,
because there is no fooling history
—we are no older than our times—
and it would not be bad. His world
contained less bad than good
that history would supersede.

"Play horsy, Mohr, play horsy!"
He could do that too, for hours on end
until the Worker State arrived
in draft with dear Herr Engels, who
would talk with Mohr deep into the night
while Jenny waited, and waited on them.

COOKING IN REVERSE

I've topped the compost pile
for winter, laid its last layers
of dried manure, soil, and ash.
With every heaping shovelful
the crooked coils of last season's
cucumber and tomato vines compress
like bedsprings. Now I've made
the bed with three coverlets,
rounded as a giant's gamy rump
asleep between four cedar posts
with draperies of chicken wire—

or as a kneaded sponge of bread.
It is a form of cooking
as of sleep. Decomposition
heats the center first,
the opposite of baking bread.
I call it cooking in reverse,
where food goes back
to its main ingredient. "Dirt
made my lunch," I heard
a first-grade chorus sing.
Now lunch makes my dirt.
And if a watched pot never boils,
I'll watch mine morning by morning,
long enough to prove
that even *never* decomposes.

Come spring I'll dish it out
in lavish, loamy helpings,
another matter
of reversals—feeding
the garden that feeds me
its first and final meal

UNLOVED

Unloved as a disfigured face,
this weed-pierced patch
of macadam by the tire shop,
this third-class commercial strip,
this seen-its-best-days
industrial town in Maine,

these down-at-heels suburbs,
these broken, fallen gutters,
these flea-market wastes,
these mangy-headed dolls

and the dogs put away in pounds
and radioactive mittens
and ulcerated membranes,
the fish no fishermen
rejoice to catch,

these menus hardly any diners
order from, their lamination peeling,
these failed, remaindered books,
failed farms, desolate views,
high tension towers,
low fashion shirts and blouses,
their plastic wrappers brittle
in the auction barn,

these untended graves,
these neon crosses,
these faded painted rocks
with "Jesus Saves,"

trite rhymes on discarded
greeting cards, attics and basements
surviving children will have to clean out,

these sagging, abandoned houses,
these saggy knees,
these knotted varicose veins,

these all-but-dead motels,
these tribes no anthropologist wants,
these Saturday doldrums,
these dusty plastic ivy leaves,

these pencils with hardened,
stained erasers and hard,
un-erasable leads, and lead
in paint, in gasoline, in sealed-off wells,

these toadstools in my basement,
these pieces of rusted wire in the ashes,
these moons of unremarkable planets,
these slippers in the kitchen trash.

Oh, Love, are you able to love them?
Oh, Love, can these dry bones live?
Oh, Love, sit down at this Formica table.
Oh, Love, bless this wonder-less bread.

DREAM ROUND

The dog barks to go out
thirty minutes before
we have to get up.

I slide to the floor
quickly, so my wife,
who chills more quickly
than I, can stay.

Back in bed,
I tuck my chin to my chest
and raise my hand
like a boxer's glove
to my pillow: now begins

the last round
of dreams, their final
blows to the head before
the bell rings and the real
blows rain down.

Gentle and close,
in my corner as always,
she breathes warm
against my neck;

I begin to breathe
more deeply now,
knocked out, but only
for the count of five.

COUPLES WHO SMOKE

I like to watch the intimacy
of couples who smoke, how deftly he gets
the lighter from her purse, how she
slips into his pocket for cigarettes—

making love so casually while
they entertain or mind the kids.
It's like a telepathic smile,
a secret shared without any words.

You say what they share is their cancers,
but the health in vogue is rarely shared.
I love these non-aerobic dancers,
outmoded, out of breath, but paired.

RAHULA

My former student is an anarchist
in the Bay Area, the gay area too.
Her three-year-old wears a T-shirt
that reads "Potential Queer."

My former student is an anarchist.
She threw a pie in the mayor's face.
For years she put out a 'zine
she christened *Progress Sucks*.

My former student is an anarchist,
more so now that she's a mom.
She calls her new 'zine *Joybringer*
in honor of her free-born kid.

My former student is an anarchist.
Once I kicked her out of class.
She's done her homework ever since,
joybringer, suckling my hopes.

OLD HIPPIES

Among the things they turned upside down,
the proverb "Only the good die young"—
true enough, musically speaking: I can't
imagine Janis Joplin feeding us yet
another piece of her heart.

                    Otherwise,
it was the good who lasted, held plumb,
stayed beautiful, beat but unbeaten, silver
manes seldom except among Apaches that
forever young. You find them at farmers' markets,
unabashedly tie-dyed, fit as their fiddles
but not to be tied, off the grid.

                    Oh,
the miles they must have traveled, the long, strange
trips, the fucking around all over the place,
though they look quite monogamous now, bagging
up the bok choy, gypsy bracelets jangling,
knuckles raw from an oil change on that still
magic bus.

                    Was it the One-a-Days
when kids, the Beaver Cleaver diet—the acid
even, playing changes on their DNA?
How stingy that sounds beside their generosity,
the way their wrinkles Crosby, Stills, and Nash
when they smile. "We are what we eat," they might
concede, expanding "Feed your head" to plug
the wares, as in "Try these organic elderberries."
But the secret's not for sale.

We are the fruit
of our refusals—in their case, to alter when
they alteration found, when the times that were
a-changin' changed right back, to spay Love's *yes*,
unsaying its litter of *no*'s: no selling out,
no buying the bull till you've bought the farm.

FOR A FRIEND ABOUT TO GIVE NOTICE

You may find the poems come harder
once you're retired.

Now you're writing one a day
and have been for years,
and for years I've been amazed
at your output.

But the Muse has been known
to take pity on a laboring man,
to favor him with a flash
of thigh as he barrows wet cement
past her high veranda.

Living with her everyday
is a different affair.

She will expect you
to set your own alarm
and rise to it without complaint,
bring her coffee and a cruller,
and pay attendance in ways
you can scarcely imagine.

She will bear you children,
daughters all
as lovely as herself,
and every one will need a dowry.

THREE DAYS IN SAVANNAH

For Kathy and Cinda

The River

Quebec, Savannah—
  my restless heart always rests
    best by a river.

Larger than life, and like
  a life, this great river barge.
    What secrets it holds!

No flying saucer
  more mysterious than this
    monolithic hull.

A tugboat muscles
  upstream like a bantamweight
    entering a bar.

Black man with a mess
  of night-caught fish at his feet,
    two mouths moving still.

One more old fellow
  benched in bright sneakers, watching
    the boats pass. Yes, me.

The Streets

Hand in hand they go,
  his long stride matched by the brisk
    pace of her wheelchair.

Irish pubs surprised
  me in Savannah, palm trees,
    New England chowder.

Air conditioners
  weep for the world's lost ozone.
    I dodge the tearfall.

I could not translate
  the evangelist's accent.
    Good he had a sign.

Music fires the night,
  torch songs, red hot blues. Shadows
    move from blaze to blaze.

The Shade

Hot cities prize trees.
  Shady lanes and graveyards made
    the Southern Gothic.

No white Christmas here,
  but Spanish moss like tinsel
    trims tradition's trees.

Setting an easel
  outdoors is taking a stand
    of sorts. A brave one.

For a good hotel,
  I'll tell you what—I'd go so
    far as to travel.

The Ancestors

Ballast from English
  ships became the cobblestones
    of Old Savannah.

Oglethorpe devised
  a city of parks planted
    with transplanted men.

John Wesley preached here,
  hating slavery before King
    Cotton or John Brown.

Refugee tombstones,
  bereft of graves. Union troops
    broke them, breaking camp.

City of pirates
  and obliging ghosts, the haunt
    of tourists tonight.

I light this candle
  for Flannery O'Connor,
    who lit dark places.

The Women

Art students tiptoe
  astride their bikes, their bare legs
    best Botticelli.

Fuck this and fuck that
  says Go-girl till the green light
    clears the air of her.

Lord, bless these bellies,
  budding, pregnant, bidding me
    conceive this blessing.

Homecoming parade,
  Savannah State: one hundred
    high-stepping black queens.

Driving to the sea,
  my wife, her friend, copilot
    a funny story.

The Sea

Our friend bags seashells
  like coins, but hold out your hand:
    She is no miser.

Surfcasting against
  an east wind, the old man reels
    the lure of pleasure.

Rare the unbroken
   shell, rare the apprehension
      of fragmentary . . .

Toddler on the beach:
   His sea legs say go before
      his brain can say where.

Shell-hunting till dusk,
   you look up to find the sky
      all mother of pearl.

NOW AND THEN

The power's been out since four a.m.,
when a thunderstorm ripped over our mountain.
All morning long I've been aware
of the silence in the house—no hum
from the refrigerator, no radio jabber,
the fish tank filter deathly still,
and since today's a holiday,
not much besides a breeze
comes down our road.

How quiet they must have been,
the days before power
became so literally a household word.
I think that sounds were sharper
against that stillness,
bird songs and piano chords,
the voice that called your name.

But thunder in the night
and the downpour's waking rush,
the window slammed like a shot
and the child crying out in dread
were the same. The mother's voice
against all godly threats, calm
among the tossing silhouettes
and phantom flashes, was
no more welcome then or less.

SHORT ADVENTURE

He was exploring the borders of fiction
when he met a woman
exploring the borders of gender,
and they set off together
to explore the borders of reality
but only got so far
as the borders of spelling,
whereupon they became boarders
of a borderline psychotic
billionaire, who liked them
though he found them bores.

Meanwhile, over the border,
just before the break of day,
just ahead of the border patrol,
came a brown man and his wife
to mow the lawns
and edge the borders
along the pathway to the pool,
where much to their surprise
they discovered the lady
of the house, the borderline
psychotic's bored-to-tears wife,
giving her borders
a Brazilian bikini wax.

That night there was a party
at the furthest borders of taste.
The boarders and the borderline
psychotic and his wife ate
the brown people with chilies
round the borders of their plates.

MY DAUGHTER'S SINGING

I will miss the sound of her singing
through the wall that separates
her bathroom from ours, in the morning
before school, how she would harmonize
with the bare-navel angst
of some screaming Ophelia on her stereo,
though she had always seemed a contented kid,
a grower of rare gourds, an aficionado
of salamanders, and a babysitter prized
for her playful, earnest care, her love
of children so pure she seemed to become
a little child whenever she took one by the hand,
entering heaven so handily.
But it reminded me, that singing,
of the soul depths we never know,
even in those we love more than our souls,
so mad we are to anticipate the future,
and already I am talking—
a year to go before she goes
to college, and listen to me talking—
in the past tense as she sings.

FIRST CRUSH

Late at night with the laughter
of lovers in the distance,
she walks like a beachcomber
or a murmuring chambermaid
picking up the crushes that strew the earth,
the innocent, hopeless crushes
of boys and girls, women and men.

Perhaps only she can remember
how they came to be called *crushes*,
for she finds them crushed
in her path each night
as if from accidents
of birth, of handsomeness,
of encounters too late or early in life—
they smell almost of blame.

She gathers them up,
smoothing their bruised petals
to the best of her ability,
which is considerable,
and holds them to her breast.

She too has had her crushes,
billions and billions,
more even than the blossoms
that she clutches like a bride's
cast-off bouquet.

THE GOOSE

And this is how the goose's goose was cooked
in the seventeenth century, alive, first plucking
all the feathers save those around the head
and neck (and the billed head turning, bewildered,
part of the twisted fun—what are they doing?
what are they going to do?—the gang rapists' kick)
then surrounding it with fire, the frantic goose
gulping the water provided to keep the meat
moist. If the animal fainted, the cook removed
it from the heat, patting and moistening the breast
above its heart. The goose must be made to survive
until the carving, so that it cried with each slice.

The West! you say, the West! That old medieval
cruelty, the Christian nightmare with its torture-loving
martyr myths, its hell of repressed lust.
So you have never heard of Chinese monkey feasts,
the table sectioned like a horizontal pillory,
the collared monkey Groucho-marched into the hall,
its neck locked into the center hole, eyes
beyond belief as the cranial cap is sawn
and lifted, the feasters spooning the living brains.

Civilization then, whether West or East! What happens
with the building of cities, the division of labor by caste,
the enslavement that makes leisure, the common wheel.
But Kalahari Bushmen love to find
a tortoise and bury it in a bed of coals, roasting
it live in its carapace. As befitting their primitive state,
apparently they eat it dead, though turtle hearts
are known to beat hours after dismemberment.

It is man then, man! I will cry uncle and his name
shall be Man—as if I'd never seen a housecat
toy the mice to death, or was nuts enough
to call it mercy because a few escape;
as if there were no times when I have felt
some respite cool my baking heart, only
to be thrust toward the flames again. How we whimper
at our carving, Love, and I want to know
what horror's in your heart. Declare yourself!
But all I hear you say . . . *I am the goose.*

"MY FIRST ESCAPE"

In my hands, I had a copy of the "Iliad"
in the Russian hexameter of Gnyeditch;
in my pocket, a passport made out in the name
of Trotsky, which I wrote in it at random,
without ever imagining that it would become
my name for the rest of my life.

Thus he makes his first escape—
from Siberia into his fixed identity.
Homer too might be a pseudonym,
might not have been one bard.
Collective authorship—the Marxist
in him must have smiled at the thought.

He believes in history
more than in himself,
is not dismayed by randomness.
A losing streak is merely that,
a streak on the windowpane
of his railway carriage speeding west.

Years later a case of flu contracted
duck hunting on the River Dubna
will keep him from Lenin's funeral
and from the struggle for succession,

as the quarrel over Brisêis,
will keep Achilles in his tent the day
when Hector nearly torched the ships.

Nearly. Homer does not bother
to tell us of the wooden horse, the arrow
in the hero's heel. He assumes we know
where all of this is going.

WEEPING WILLOW BLUES

That weeping willow sure
is a lachrymose tree—
I mean the big one at our house,
tin-sliver tears all over the place,
stuck in the lettuces
and littering the lawn.
My rake is a busy handkerchief,
I'll tell you that,
and the dropped dry eyelashes,
I have to clean those up too
and once in a while lift up
a fallen limb. If the trunk
ever goes, it's likely that's the end
of our kitchen. Another man
would have had it down by now,
but all that dappled smooching,
so cool under its hang-down hair,
and its crazy hula in a storm
make me want it very much
to outlive me. Anyway,
the wood's no good for burning,
and if I didn't have to rake,
what else would I do, what else
find to moan over? Listening now
to Lightnin' Hopkins,
I ask old Lightnin' for some light.
Weepin' willow like a woman,
he tells me, *bother you all day long.*
Weepin' willow like a woman,
bother you all day long.
But if she ever go and leave you,
you be cryin' a weepin' willow song.

THE WORLD PUSHES BACK

Lift me, says the suitcase
and makes my hand
magnetic with the ground.
Pull me, says the starter rope,
and pulls me yet again
out of the mind's dark well.
Resist me, says your back
pressed against mine
in the night, so firm it is
almost irresistible.

NEW LACES

How is it that I take such pure delight
in new boot laces?
I doubt an ocean cruise
would please me more
than cutting those old lines away,
unthreadable otherwise,
so knotted they've become
from my repairs—cut free,
and all the eyes open.
I thread the new one through
the lowest two,
adjusting the lengths so their tips touch
as equals, as bride and groom
who now may kiss
then part to weave their sovereign lives
in crisscross till they emerge
much shortened but equal still.
How neat to pull them tight,
no thin-ice hesitance when
I snug up the boot; nothing breaks
in the fellowship of the foot
with the nut and screw—
then that perfect bow,
as if my feet were wedding gifts, as if
there's no "as if," so sure I stand.

MAKING LOVE TO MEDUSA

The approach perforce is from the rear,
the full force of her face turned away.
No modesty was ever more severe.

The snakes bear watching
and are themselves on watch.
He waves his hand and makes them sway.
Not one strand is out of place.
No two of them so much as touch.

Dipping splayed fingers like a comb,
he squeezes their bodies tight, almost to death.
Their mouths gape and she goes to her knees.
He strokes her scaly flesh,
so like the chapped, escaping moan
she begs herself to suppress.

Only her scalp is undefiled
by the jealous curse,
smooth as silk between the reptiled
roots, the radiance that was hers.

Now no ugliness he sees
save that of the offended god,
whose cruelty so unmans him
that only by the turning of her face
can she make him hard.

1917

No diesel engines then
to make steam locomotives quaint,
no Holocaust to dwarf
the Hun atrocities in Belgium,

no digitally mastered sound
to amplify the phonograph
needle's scratch, no new wave
of emancipated women issuing

from the underground, hailing taxis,
to vindicate the eccentric suffragist.
Like now, it was only the present.
The future was a distant star

whose light had not arrived;
nostalgia had nothing pertinent to say
in the newspapers, and time healed
nothing that was hurting at the time.

STRAIT IS THE WAY

A phrase in Gide—"a serenity that was
very like happiness"—grips me hard, first
by the closeness of the two, like bee and buzz;
and then, that they are not the same, a burst

of recognition for one who walks among
his humming blooms musing, "I'm happy." He means,
doesn't he, that nothing can be too wrong
with the world if he's allowed his old routines.

Too simple, that. I'm also loved, employed
in work I love, enjoy my wine and diet
with grace, my honey penned from a life enjoyed.
My happiness is surely more than quiet.

Yet who was it said, "Happy are they who mourn"?
Who dared to tell the happy they must be reborn?

BEFORE FALLING ASLEEP

The rain on the cathedral stones,
the traveler's dream of rain,
the swollen stream under the arched
stone bridge, the damp tweed
and the glistening black umbrellas,
the crisp letters pressed black
into the parchment of the poet's
slender golden volume, like a playbill
in heaven, the illuminating curves
of every last supper's candle flames—
all are joined in the settle of your flesh
against me, and for me, your softest
sigh. O Lamb of God, we come
through all the dearest places we have gone.
And we come so swiftly.

OUR PARENTS' STAMINA

We marveled at our parents' stamina,
their stoic calm when we were bored and young—
how they could stand the heat in berry patches
and strip chicken carcasses down to the last
scrap, wait in beach-bound traffic and not cry,
endure a tie and swallow medicines
and oratory sitting still—afraid
but sure in time they'd teach the art to us.

We did not know that it was we who taught
the art to them, how to snap alert from sleep
and place the blistered nipple in our mouths,
hold back their tears at our vaccinations, hush
their hurried passion's climax—we did not know
how we had turned them into stones that love.

PINK CARNATIONS

Pink carnations in a milk-white vase
with green, green stems and leaves
stand out on the shelf
under the kitchen windows,
pink against the sunlit snow.

They would be outdoors if they could.
They would go toward the snow
as much as they go with the snow,
the pinkness of their edges nearly white.

Once our daughter stood by this same shelf,
a handhold when she learned to stand.
She hummed and colored pictures there
and looked out at the world
and the cold, cold snow.

FOR SARAH, ON HER WAY TO ROCK POINT

Rock of Ages, cleft for me . . .

Everyone older or younger than you, counselors
in college, campers young as six, you twenty-
six, I can imagine you telling a tale in the firelight:
"Once there was a girl under a witch's spell,
and whatever age she happened to be, no one
else was that same age. On the day she was born,
no others were born, and though others would die
on the day of her death, none would have her dates
carved with their epitaph, no one blow
as many candles out on a cake as she."
And so on. I don't believe in witches, of course,
or spells; I only find it hard to believe
you're twenty-six (your mother and I, fifty-
seven), inasmuch as that means anything.
No one on this earth, not even a twin,
is as old as anyone else; no one has the same
number of gray hairs or heartaches, has read
an equal number of pages with a comprehension
matching yours. Our ages are unique
as snowflakes, as individual as our DNA.
Two Rip Van Winkles wake up having dreamt
different dreams. Still, they might find subjects
of common concern to talk about, where
to go for a haircut, how to burnish a rusted gun.
And so will you. While watching for the signs
inviting conversation, be sure you see
those sights so old that dating them takes science:
granite outcrops, moonlit cresting waves,

the overarching trees that comb the sunlight.
Our pleasure in them makes us contemporary
with cave people, who touch our hands across
millennia, as you will, climbing, reaching out
toward help or need, not always knowing
the difference or caring to, the rock being the point.

WOLF HALL

It will take a little courage
to finish this book
that I do not want to end.
I ration the pages
as on certain nights
I ration love,
but passion draws us on.

This life too—
my woods, my work,
to see the garden through
to the stripped harvest.
I can't even imagine
my last look at the sea.

But we must see
the story to its end;
our passion draws us on.
We lust for the finish.

It takes courage to live,
they tell me, which is true,
though some of it comes
down to the courage not to.

FOR THOSE WHO TALK OF GROWTH

On the first warm day in spring
(no, not the first, but the first
warm Sunday after the snow
had melted off the banks
along the road—see how
I tend to simplify—)

I raked sand the snowplow
had thrown up on our lawn
down into the ditch, or away,
with a quick, slinging stroke,
into the bordering brush.

I had clean grass and a thought,
a symbol of my growth.
The sand is what served me
for a time, some friend, some
creed that gave me traction
once, but now only burdens
the life I must rake free of it.

So nice. But I have moved
the sand, not voided it.
Nor am I done with snow.
It will come and I shall go
nowhere without the sand.

FIRST AFRICAN

Georgia, 1855

A humdrum *via dolorosa*,
this women's work of bearing
manmade bricks up from the riverside
barefoot over cobblestone streets

to build a church for slaves,
the drum distant in memory,
the hum close by in the Savannah heat,
a humdrum way of tears

familiar in the brick-making
of Joseph's captive descendents—
"Out of Egypt have I called my son,"
whose feet also would bleed

on slave-ship ballast emptied out
and spread for paving stones: bones, names,
and sundry redemptions mixed like sand
in the mortar of unhealing time.

Time was, free time was for hiring out
oneself for wages, put aside grain
by grain to purchase freedom—that promise
now squandered for beams and nails

to build a church for slaves,
in their free night hours less free

than they were before—and more so,
the sacrifice of freedom freely chosen

for a humdrum *via dolorosa*,
the drum beating in the chest
and the hum like honey in the mouth
clenched tight against the bruising climb,

every woman her own Veronica,
wiping sweat with a kerchief also her own.
Hers too the still-born, back-borne pregnancy,
man-formed bricks like the first man

formed in God's image, flesh of the King
who took upon himself the form of a slave,
that at the mention of his name
every knee shall refuse to bow

under its yoke—and did refuse
in the prescient, backward-casting change
of name from "First Colored" to "First African,"
recalling sinless Lucy, mother of Mary and Eve,

mothers of this handsome son, the "I-am
your-tour-guide-today," who tells us,
when his father had the heart attack, the pastor
called and asked about his schoolwork,

there being no father left on earth to ask.
If you could hear him now, thou

brick-bearing, master-suckling mothers,
recount your stations in his filial pride,

would you say your sacrifice was worth it?
Or would you tell us not to ask
eternal questions heaven alone can bear,
lacking which there is no sacrifice?

NORTH EASTER

I always go to town, loving
to go, when a blizzard is predicted.
The milk of human kindness glistens
on the nipples of disaster.
No one shows up at the lost and found
to claim his enemy.
Deep down we are all preparing
to meet our Maker, no less
poignantly than our hibernator's panic
empties the supermarket shelves
of toilet paper, candles, milk, and wine.
Never mind that they'll have it all plowed in a day—
some old wrinkle in the brain keeps whispering
Ice Age, while the winking stem
goes into heat. You will remember
the famous New York City Blackout,
how nine months later the maternity wards
were crowded as a rush-hour train. Just think
of all the babies that will start tonight
with the snow already starting to fall
like the sperm of angels, and it looks
as though more than one is getting through
to the egg. Forget biology, man;
this is metaphysics. This is the eve
of our great North Easter, when the world
awakes inside the hillside petals
of a single gleaming lily, dusted
with the pollen of the risen sun.

BARTLEBY

Bartleby preferred not to.
I prefer to defer to

my betters who want the best.
I'm quite happy with the rest.

You take the e-mail.
I'll settle for snail.

You click.
I'll lick

the envelope.
You be the pope,

I'll be the paisan
of information.

Cybersex? No, no, you go ahead.
I'll stay here with my Luddite, in bed.

A SONG FOR ELEANOR

You ate their resentment.
You drank their dislike.
They called you Jew-lover,
And they called you a dyke,
A disgrace to your sex,
A traitor to your class.
They made fun of your face.
They made fun of your ass.
But, Eleanor, Eleanor, you were a beautiful woman.

An awkward girl
With unfortunate teeth,
Your heart in your throat
And your hair in a wreath,
A debutante martyr
Who would know the knife
Of the backward glance
At the President's wife.
But, Eleanor, Eleanor, you were a beautiful woman.

I can see the moment
When you held your breath,
When you saw your situation
And foresaw your death,
And that there ain't no loss
And there ain't no gain.
All that counts
Is the relief of pain.
Yeah, Eleanor, Eleanor, you were a beautiful woman.

So get the shop girl
And the refugee
And the Pullman porter
And invite 'em to tea.
Take the cup of squalor
And the pinch of hate,
Mix 'em up and put 'em
On the President's plate.
Oh, Eleanor, Eleanor, you were a beautiful woman.

Up in heaven
where the Wobblies are
And the saints' communion
Is a working class bar,
And the waiters all sit
And the cripples all fly,
You can hear 'em whisper
When you walk by:
"Eleanor, Eleanor, you are a beautiful woman."

WAITING

I'm beginning to believe what the scriptures tell.
Bob Dylan.

Life is not like Beckett.
Only Beckett is like Beckett.
This is much to Beckett's credit
but in no wise to life's blame.

Most of us are not waiting for Godot.
We're waiting for the toast to pop,
the cross-town bus to arrive,
the talker in the row behind us
to get interested enough in the picture
to finally for the love of Christ shut up.

It is amazing, really, how un-amazing it is
that most of the things we wait for come.
(The bigmouth is handed a behemoth
bucket of pacifying popcorn.
It seems that she was waiting too.)
Not the things we fear, and certainly not
the things we conjure, but the things we wait for
honestly—most of them come. Even soldiers,
waited for and after a time given up for dead,
appear once in a while, gaunt impossibilities
at a second husband's door.

One of the most amazing phenomena many of us
know, an orgasm, is pretty much a wait that can wait
no longer. It comes—so wonderfully that people will say
that they did. *They* came. There is philosophy in that.

And babies, still more wonderful than orgasms,
also cry out and are waited for, and also mostly come.

There is nothing like this in Beckett,
one reason that of all the great dramatists
he is the least prone to make me horny.
(Don't you find the theater makes you horny?)
I want to call him chaste but that's not it,
because chastity can make us horny too.
Something else: Wait. It will come to me.

Sometimes I am in my backyard waiting
for the garden to look saturated, sated
under the swaying nozzle of my hose,
or for paint to dry, or for the burgers to brown,
and it strikes me how the trumpet may sound
and the dead may be raised incorruptible, perhaps
for no other reason than that people were waiting for it,
that a second coming will seem no more than medium
    rare,

when the Son of man appears in the clouds
as remarkable as but no more remarkable
than a hot air balloon rising over the mountain.
In fact some people will say, "Hey, look!
There's a hot air balloon rising over the mountain.
That face looks so familiar. Wait, wait, don't tell me."
At Rushmore they will think it's another president.
But when the tribes of the earth begin to wail
theory flies out the window.

Those of us who preferred theater to theory
and ceremony to belief, who found our clearest window
between those painted drapes, will exclaim,
"This just can't be happening! This is just
too absurd!" till rising from the ground, beginning
with a flattop haircut, the lined mug of an Irish play-
  wright
will say, "That's mainly what I was trying to tell you,"

which will be true enough, but only in a minor way,
the main truth being that it wasn't in the least—

absurd, I mean.

Only a few minutes late, the bus pulls to the curb
and the man who steps up with his token,
still reading his newspaper,
does not feel mocked by the hissing of the doors.

CONFESSION

The month is only two days old and already
we have seen a circus
and ridden a bicycle together.

I wish I had never told a lie in my life

CLEARING THE AIR

My father bought the best
air purifiers he could find,
hoping they would ease the nighttime
scratching in his throat,
whatever airborne irritant
would take him from the phone
coughing like mad, not knowing
this was the asbestosis
that would cut off his oxygen
and eventually his life, not before
putting him out of his mind—

not knowing, I said, as the Navy didn't
know when it padded the destroyer
on which he served with the friable
fibers that would wreck his breath.

They thought they were protecting
the sailors from a fiery death,
and they were more or less right,
as my father was in thinking
his devices cleared the air

of present particles, but not
of past, nor of the irony that laughs
alike at peace and war,
at the lies we tell in our right minds
and the truths we utter raving.

LIKE CHURCH

Only after leaving Portland did I realize
we had never seen the sea.

We had walked out on a wharf,
eaten lobster in a shipshape pound
on pilings, and climbed the narrow
cobble streets in a salted mist.

Fishing boats and even a yacht
were moored along the quay in what
must surely have been sea water.

But the sea we never saw.

We only knew its presence
everywhere, vague fulfillment
of the longing we had felt
when setting out, we told
ourselves, to see the sea.

A FLASH OF LITHE WHITE ARMS

A flash of lithe white arms
and legs farther up the road,
quick from behind a tall hedge,
retrieving a bounce-away ball—

"Nausikaa with her white arms flashing,"
as Homer sang it nearly
three thousand years ago—

then vanishing just as quick,
tells me how the myth
of nymphs began in a twilight
glimpse of skin or snatch
of distant girlish laughter

told as something magical,
if only to evoke the mere
and perfect original.

THE CARLYLES GET A SECOND CHANCE

After their conference with the doctor,
they decided they would put off
consummation for a while,
not for the probable two score
years of their previous life,
but at least for a day or so.

The first night he allowed his hand
to venture up her nightdress
to just above her ticklish knee.
The next night she allowed herself
to enjoy where it came to rest.
The third night she cried aloud,
frightening them both until
she smiled and stroked his hand.

The fourth they came together
at last, the fifth and sixth also,
and on the seventh night they rested,
knowing they'd soon have the knack.

In a year came their first child,
and two years later the decision
that Jane should acquire a job.

She got a breast pump
and a briefcase, a nanny
who could cook some things passably well.
Thomas got promoted at the university,

came close to failing a peer-reviewed
affair and about as close to forgiveness.

He never finished *The French Revolution.*
Years later he would say that Mill,
or Mill's maid or mistress, whoever
had tossed the damn thing into the fire,
had done him the greatest favor of his life.
Asked to write on the burning
question of American slavery,
he answered, "Why not ask Mill?
He's better at the burning stuff."

Jane, meanwhile, discovered
she was good with cameras,
much in vogue at the time.
She might have set up a studio,
but for the kids and her reluctance
to give up the regular paycheck.

No lesbian novelists or Italian radicals
came to adore her, and Leigh Hunt
and Ralph Emerson never came to call.
Thomas never got the chance to ask
Darwin if men turned back to apes.
He and Jane had other friends,
not at all famous but only
a little less interesting,
the same being true for them.

They were happier, he and she.
It's hard to say if they were better off
or what that mattered in the end.
God loved them just as much
as in their first-draft life,
and they were just as unaware.

THE PEARL

I find your bracelet,
the one with the pink pearls
or whatever they are—something
neither real nor fake I never understood—
the one I gave you for Christmas, lying
unclasped on the kitchen table
after you've left for work.

I know why it's there.
You'd meant for me to help you
latch it, as I do some mornings,
but I'd already gone outside
to my frostier chores,
taking some of your equipment
to the car, then taking a kiss
when you passed by wishing
me a quiet, uninterrupted day.

How I wanted to ride to where you work,
stride into your office unannounced,
latch your bracelet on your wrist,
Galahad your Monday, gallop away!

But I would only have embarrassed you,
turned your cheeks as pink as these,
and made your wish, dear
as the purest pearl to me, of no account.

PROBABLY NOT THIS ONE

You will, if the gods allow,
produce six to ten poems
that mortals will remember,
and to do this you may
need to write thousands,
and even millions
are no guarantee.

Six to ten.
It might even be one
or what rhymes with one.

Then again you may write
the great six straight off
without being written off—
it happens—

and happily go sailing off
under the Rimbaud rainbow
or scribbling tripe
till a ripe old age.

There is no way to know
this or most any *this*.
Or *that* for that matter.
It is not for you
to know the times or the seasons,
but to set your face toward Jerusalem,

Athens, or let us say Paterson,
where babies are waiting
to be delivered, lovers to be
loved, an opus ever opening
for you at the Falls.

COUSIN RICK

1.
He was becoming a monk,
my distant cousin Rick,
son of my mother's
distant cousin Jean, not a Catholic
monk, it was quickly added,
but Episcopal, which is sort of
like Catholic but without the Pope.
I barely understood
the difference or what it meant
to be a monk, was still a bit tentative
on the concept of cousin.

2.
My parents had a glimpse of Rick
at a family gathering out west,
though not so west as cowboys.
He was a novice then
in the Order of St. Francis,
and I, a novice in the order of kid.

Forever taking down or pinning up
the cuffs of my Sunday suit,
my mother duly noted his high-water pants,
hand-me-downs he wore
to keep his vow of poverty.

3.
I fancied being a minister
as a child, then a missionary,
as more bold, and to be bolder

still, to go as far away
as New Guinea,
"the wildest place on earth,"
where the deer and the cannibals play.

So when Rick became, not only a monk,
but a missionary to New Guinea,
while I became, not only an Episcopalian,
but a savage parish priest,
neither with benefit
of the other's influence,
it was as if we were related
by a water thicker than blood.

4.
We met for the first time
at my parents' surprise
fiftieth anniversary party,
both of us shy
of middle age,
though he seemed far beyond
the usual passages, dressed
in a suit that fit him to a T
and in the color that goes
with everything, fully prepared
to celebrate a milestone
on the road he had not taken,
attentive to his mother and to mine.

5.
He had first gone to New Guinea

on sabbatical, already a monk
living by the rule and doubtless
well-acquainted with irony,

though one has to wonder
which takes the bigger cake:
going to New Guinea
for your year of rest,
or hearing a call to serve
there while you rested.

6.
The second and only other time
we met was in New York
at a diner on lower Eighth
in between my sit-down with an editor
and his with his support group.
He wore a straw hat, sandals,
and carried a Papuan shoulder bag
that got glances even in that joint.

What touched me more than where he'd been
in the last years, or in that last hour,
was where he was headed after breakfast:
to buy more guppies.

The first batch, he told me, had died
during his last time out in the field.
His brothers at the mother house
(his brothers!)
hadn't bothered to feed them.

7.
The news comes shortly after Advent,
perhaps a day or so after
his sudden death, from heart attack
in the mountains of New Guinea.
My father thinks it would be nice
if I gave his mother a call.

"Not one myself," she says,
"I'm not sure how Episcopalians
handle these things,"
but thinks that a little portion
of his ashes ought to remain
at the Papuan school where he taught.
"They will need some closure too."

So kindly in her provision, as though
the monk were mother to the mom.

8.
His Christmas card was always our first.
He signed it "Cousin Rick" beneath the formal
Brother Justus, sometimes enclosing
the newsletter from Little Portion,
his priory on Long Island.

Justus, I remember, was the man
who drew the loser's lot
when the Apostles divined
a replacement for Judas—
a choice of name, if it was Rick's choice,
as far gone as New Guinea, and if not

his choice, then farther still.

9.
He had been in Vietnam—
that's what his obit said, "Vietnam vet,"
news to my parents and to me.
Corpsman? Chaplain? An early challenge
to his monkish bent, or the crucible
that forged his vows? Too late now to ask.

What some men would
have gotten into every
other sentence: only another indulgence
he had renounced.

10.
His Papuan protégé,
presumably the one who'd closed his eyes,
wrote to his mother, my mother's cousin Jean.

There were three villages to visit that day,
all on foot, three villages and three refrains,
as in a parable or a joke.

Attaining each one, the younger man implored,
"You're not feeling well. Let us stop here."
And Rick would answer, "No,
they are expecting us.
We must not disappoint them."

Even the helicopter came too late
to second-guess his decision.

ALL I KNOW

In the end all I know
about death
is that I shall no longer
drive a car
with my right hand
resting
on your cool, bare thigh
and that I do not
want to die.

THE LAST MAN WHO KNEW EVERYTHING

"the Jesuit scholar Athanasius Kircher (d. 1680), reputed
to be 'the last man who knew everything.'"

Some days I feel it coming,
though I do not know
the moment it will come:
the bittersweet escape
of whatever detail will inevitably
escape me—with my own escape
as a consequence.

❧

Do I know the words to every song,
or why fools fall in love,
or why the most desired men
are often fools?

Do I know what Job could never know,
the "storehouse of the hail" and all the rest,
or if I'll ever be like Job, so cursed or blessed?

❧

It comforts them to think of my omniscience
and spares them too
from further thinking and from giving
me another thought.

❧

The Last Man Who Knew Everything
does not know where he left his spectacles;
and in whatever place he finds them
he will not know why
he did not look there first.

ᕦ

The Last Man Who Knew Everything
is a celibate bore.
The First Man Who Knew Everything
knew a woman
knew more.

ᕦ

A young girl brings us eggs and cheeses.
Dark-haired she is, with rings in her ears.
I have never spoken to her,
but I have heard her singing
to her horse. This is something
I thought you'd like to know.

ᕦ

Here is something I would like to know:
when that knuckle-headed novice
is coming with my soup.

ᕦ

The Last Man Who Knew Everything—
yet I could not tell you
the first man who said so.

༦

An accolade is like a gift of magic clothes.
A myth, its effect is also mythical:
You put it on only to discover
you can't take it off,
the fit so delectable
it eats up your life.

༦

When one man can know everything—
take it as a given—such are times
when few men know much.

Yet something sweet, I think,
to live in times when *know-it-all*
is not said in derision.

༦

Maybe I do know, maybe I do.
It has occurred to me that maybe I do.
Is it my knowledge that's ironic,
or my self-deprecation?
The only thing
that is never ironic
is the need for salvation.

∾

In the best world every man
would know everything
that was worth knowing
and would know that others knew
as well as he, and would also know
that things worth knowing are few.

∾

Am I in the old world or the new?
Here's the New World on a map.
They've yet to kill a witch there,
though I happen to know they will.

∾

Omniscience is like any other job,
you do it or you don't.
You're never as proficient as supposed,
or guilty as accused,
or happy as you used to think you'd be.

∾

The Last Man Who Knew Everything
might take a nap. Then what will he know?
Not even that he's napping. Wake me
when the fools are wise or supper's come.

ACKNOWLEDGMENTS

Some of the poems in this volume first appeared in the
following journals:

AGNI: "The Last Man Who Knew Everything"
Alaska Quarterly Review: "Marx's Family"
The American Journal of Poetry: "Short Adventure"
The Antioch Review: "My First Escape"
Ascent: "Wolf Hall"
The Atlanta Review: "Old Hippies," "Probably Not This One"
Blue Unicorn: "Couples Who Smoke"
B O D Y: "Waiting"
The Carleton Miscellany: "Confession"
Cold Mountain Review: "Our Parents' Stamina"
december: "Two Trees"
descant: "For a Friend About to Give Notice"
Free State Review: "Beatrice"
Harvard Review: "First African"
The Hudson Review: "1917," "The Goose," "A Song for Eleanor"
Hunger Mountain: "The Stars Are Near"
Image: "The Details," "Hell and Love,"* "Morning"
JuxtaProse Literary Magazine: "The Sea" from "Three Days in
Savannah"
Ladowich: "All I Know," "Dream Round"
Measure: "Strait Is the Way"
The New Yorker: "When the Snake Became a Man"
Northern Woodlands: "The Neighbors"
Pegasus: "When You're Gone"
Peregrine: "My Daughter's Singing"
Plains Poetry Journal: "Leafleting with Father Castle"**
Ploughshares: "Traveling Light"
Plume Poetry: "A Flash of Lithe White Arms"

continued from previous page

Raritan: "Bartleby," "Before Falling Asleep"
The Same: "Now and Then"
Snowy Egret: "For Sarah, On Her Way to Rock Point," "For
    Those Who Talk of Growth," "North Easter"
Southwest Review: "Wind Trumps the World"
Spiritus: "First Crush"
Texas Review: "Oldsmobile," "Unloved"
Tribeca Poetry Review: "New Laces"

*Reprinted in *The Best American Poetry 2005*, edited by
    David Lehman and Paul Muldoon
**Reprinted in *A New England Sampler*, a special issue of
    Texas Review, edited by Paul Ruffin